MW01025968

THE ESSENCE OF PROGRESS AND POVERTY

DOVER THRIFT EDITIONS

Henry George

Foreword by John Dewey

DOVER PUBLICATIONS, INC.
MINEOLA, NEW YORK

DOVER THRIFT EDITIONS

General Editor: Susan L. Rattiner

Editor of This Volume: Michael Croland

Bibliographical Note

This Dover edition, first published in 2020, is an unabridged republication of *Significant Paragraphs from Progress and Poverty*, which was originally published by Doubleday, Doran & Company, Inc., Garden City, New York, in 1928. The work contains excerpts from *Progress and Poverty*, which was originally published by E. P. Dutton & Company, New York, in 1879.

Library of Congress Cataloging-in-Publication Data

Names: George, Henry, 1839–1897, author.
Title: The essence of Progress and poverty / Henry George ; foreword by
  John Dewey.
Other titles: Progress and poverty. Selections
Description: Mineola, New York : Dover Publications, Inc., 2020. | Series: Dover
  thrift editions | "This Dover edition, first published in 2020, is an unabridged
  republication of Significant Paragraphs from Progress and Poverty, which was
  originally published by Doubleday, Doran & Company, Inc., Garden City,
  New York, in 1928." | Summary: "In this brief text, John Dewey compiled
  excerpts from Henry George's influential work on economics. Fifteen chapters
  of highlights from the influential treatise"—Provided by publisher.
Identifiers: LCCN 2019041077 | ISBN 9780486842073 (paperback)
Subjects: LCSH: Economics. | Single tax.
Classification: LCC HB171 .G275 2020 | DDC 330—dc23
LC record available at https://lccn.loc.gov/2019041077

Manufactured in the United States by LSC Communications
84207X01
www.doverpublications.com

2 4 6 8 10 9 7 5 3 1

2020

Contents

AN APPRECIATION OF HENRY GEORGE

It was a happy thought of Professor Brown to select and arrange passages from Henry George's immortal work that give the gist of his contribution to political economy and social philosophy, while the pages which follow show that the task has been executed with a skill equal to the idea. The fact that Henry George has an ardent group of disciples who have a practical program for reform of taxation has tended to obscure from the recognition of students of social theory that his is one of the great names among the world's social philosophers. It would require less than the fingers of the two hands to enumerate those who from Plato down rank with him. Were he a native of some European country, it is safe to assert that he would long ago have taken the place upon the roll of the world's thinkers which belongs to him, irrespective, moreover, of adherence to his practical plan. But for some reason we Americans are slow to perceive and celebrate intellectual claims in comparison with the merits of inventors, political leaders, and great industrialists. In the case of the author of "Progress and Poverty" the failure has doubtless been accentuated in academic circles by the fact that Henry George thought, wrote, and worked outside of them. And in the world at large, in spite of the fact that no works on political economy have had the circulation and reading obtained by his writings, discussion of the practical merits of his plan of reform of taxation has actually tended to blur his outstanding position as a thinker. This has been the case because the enormous inertia of social habit and the force of tremendous vested interests have depreciated his intellectual claims in order to strengthen opposition to his practical measures.

I do not say these things in order to vaunt his place as a thinker in contrast with the merits of his proposals for a change in methods of distributing the burdens of taxation. To my mind the two things go together. His clear intellectual insight into social conditions, his passionate feeling for the remediable ills from which humanity suffers, find their logical conclusion in his plan for liberating labor and capital from the shackles which now bind them. But I am especially concerned in connection with Professor Brown's clear and well-ordered summary, to point out the claims which his social theory has upon the attention of students. No man, no graduate of a higher educational institution, has a right to regard himself as an educated man in social thought unless he has some first-hand acquaintance with the theoretical contribution of this great American thinker.

This is not the time and place, nor is there need, to dwell upon the nature of this contribution. Henry George is as clear as he is eloquent. But I cannot refrain from pointing out one feature of his thought which is too often ignored:— his emphasis upon ideal factors of life, upon what are sometimes called the imponderables. It is a poor version of his ideas which insists only upon the material effect of increase of population in producing the material or monetary increment in the value of land. One has only to read the third section of these extracts to note that Henry George puts even greater stress upon the fact that community life increases land value because it opens "a wider, fuller, and more varied life," so that the desire to share in the higher values which the community brings with it is a decisive factor in raising the rental value of land. And it is because the present system not only depresses the material status of the mass of the population, but especially because it renders one-sided and inequitable the people's share in these higher values that we find in "Progress and Poverty" the analysis of the scientist combined with the sympathies and aspirations of a great lover of mankind. There have been economists of great repute who in their pretension to be scientific have ignored the most significant elements in human nature. There have been others who were emotionally stirred by social ills and who proposed glowing schemes of betterment, but who passed lightly over facts. It is the thorough fusion of insight into actual facts and forces, with recognition of their bearing upon what makes human life worth living, that constitutes Henry George one of the world's great social philosophers.

JOHN DEWEY
October 1927

1

THE PROBLEM

COULD A FRANKLIN or a Priestley have seen, in a vision of the future, the steamship taking the place of the sailing vessel, the railroad train of the wagon, the reaping machine of the scythe, the threshing machine of the flail; could he have heard the throb of the engines that in obedience to human will, and for the satisfaction of human desire, exert a power greater than that of all the men and all the beasts of burden of the earth combined; could he have seen the forest tree transformed into finished lumber—into doors, sashes, blinds, boxes or barrels, with hardly the touch of a human hand; the great workshops where boots and shoes are turned out by the case with less labor than the old-fashioned cobbler could have put on a sole; the factories where, under the eye of a girl, cotton becomes cloth faster than hundreds of stalwart weavers could have turned it out with their hand-looms; could he have seen steam hammers shaping mammoth shafts and mighty anchors, and delicate machinery making tiny watches; the diamond drill cutting through the heart of the rocks, and coal oil sparing the whale; could he have realized the enormous saving of labor resulting from improved facilities of exchange and communication—sheep killed in Australia eaten fresh in England, and the order given by the London banker in the afternoon executed in San Francisco in the morning of the same day; could he have conceived of the hundred thousand improvements which these only suggest, what would he have inferred as to the social condition of mankind?

It would not have seemed like an inference; further than the vision went it would have seemed as though he saw; and his heart would have leaped and his nerves would have thrilled, as one who from a height beholds just ahead of the thirst-stricken caravan the living gleam of rustling woods and the glint of laughing waters. Plainly, in the sight of the imagination, he would have beheld these new forces elevating society from its very foundations, lifting the very poorest above the possibility of want, exempting the very lowest from anxiety for the material needs of life; he would have seen these slaves of the lamp of knowledge taking on themselves the traditional curse, these muscles of iron and sinews of steel making the poorest laborer's life a holiday, in which every high quality and noble impulse could have scope to grow.

And out of these bounteous material conditions he would have seen arising, as necessary sequences, moral conditions realizing the golden age of which mankind always dreamed. Youth no longer stunted and starved; age no longer harried by avarice; the child at play with the tiger; the man with the muck-rake drinking in the glory of the stars! Foul things fled, fierce things tame; discord turned to harmony! For how could there be greed where all had enough? How could the vice, the crime, the ignorance, the brutality, that spring from poverty and the fear of poverty, exist where poverty had vanished? Who should crouch where all were freemen; who oppress where all were peers?

More or less vague or clear, these have been the hopes, these the dreams born of the improvements which give this wonderful era its preëminence. They have sunk so deeply into the popular mind as radically to change the currents of thought, to recast creeds and displace the most fundamental conceptions. The haunting visions of higher possibilities have not merely gathered splendor and vividness, but their direction has changed—instead of seeing behind the faint tinges of an expiring sunset, all the glory of the daybreak has decked the skies before.

It is true that disappointment has followed disappointment, and that discovery upon discovery, and invention after invention, have neither lessened the toil of those who most need respite, nor brought plenty to the poor. But there have been so many things to which it seemed this failure could be laid, that faith has hardly weakened. We have better appreciated the difficulties to be overcome; but not the less trusted that the tendency of the times was to overcome them.

Now, however, we are coming into collision with facts which there can be no mistaking. From all parts of the civilized world come complaints of industrial depression; of labor condemned to involuntary idleness; of capital massed and wasting; of pecuniary distress among business men; of want and suffering and anxiety among the working classes. All the dull, deadening pain, all the keen, maddening anguish, that to great masses of men are involved in the words "hard times," have afflicted the world. This state of things, common to communities differing so widely in situation, in political institutions, in fiscal and financial systems, in density of population and in social organization, can hardly be accounted for by local causes. There is distress where large standing armies are maintained, but there is also distress where the standing armies are nominal; there is distress where protective tariffs stupidly and wastefully hamper trade, but there is also distress where trade is nearly free; there is distress where autocratic government yet prevails, but there is also distress where

political power is wholly in the hands of the people; in countries where paper is money, and in countries where gold and
silver are the only currency. Evidently, beneath all such things
as these, we must infer a common cause.

That there is a common cause, and that it is either what we
call material progress or something closely connected with
material progress, becomes more than an inference when it is
noted that the phenomena we class together and speak of as
industrial depression are but intensifications of phenomena
which always accompany material progress, and which show
themselves more clearly and strongly as material progress
goes on.

It has always been to the newer countries—that is, to the
countries where material progress is yet in its earlier stages—
that laborers have emigrated in search of higher wages, and
capital has flowed in search of higher interest. It is in the older
countries—that is to say, the countries where material progress has reached later stages—that widespread destitution is
found in the midst of the greatest abundance. Go into a new
community where Anglo-Saxon vigor is just beginning the
race of progress; where the machinery of production and
exchange is yet rude and inefficient; where the increment of
wealth is not yet great enough to enable any class to live in
ease and luxury; where the best house is but a cabin of logs
or a cloth and paper shanty, and the richest man is forced to
daily work—and though you will find an absence of wealth
and all its concomitants, you will find no beggars. There
is no luxury, but there is no destitution. No one makes an
easy living, nor a very good living; but every one *can* make a
living, and no one able and willing to work is oppressed by
the fear of want.

But just as such a community realizes the conditions which
all civilized communities are striving for, and advances in the

scale of material progress—just as closer settlement and a more intimate connection with the rest of the world, and greater utilization of labor-saving machinery, make possible greater economies in production and exchange, and wealth in consequence increases, not merely in the aggregate, but in proportion to population—so does poverty take a darker aspect. Some get an infinitely better and easier living, but others find it hard to get a living at all. The "tramp" comes with the locomotive, and almshouses and prisons are as surely the marks of "material progress" as are costly dwellings, rich warehouses, and magnificent churches. Upon streets lighted with gas and patrolled by uniformed policemen, beggars wait for the passer-by, and in the shadow of college, and library, and museum, are gathering the more hideous Huns and fiercer Vandals of whom Macaulay prophesied.

This fact—the great fact that poverty and all its concomitants show themselves in communities just as they develop into the conditions toward which material progress tends—proves that the social difficulties existing wherever a certain stage of progress has been reached, do not arise from local circumstances, but are, in some way or another, engendered by progress itself.

And, unpleasant as it may be to admit it, it is at last becoming evident that the enormous increase in productive power which has marked the present century and is still going on with accelerating ratio, has no tendency to extirpate poverty or to lighten the burdens of those compelled to toil. It simply widens the gulf between Dives and Lazarus, and makes the struggle for existence more intense. The march of invention has clothed mankind with powers of which a century ago the boldest imagination could not have dreamed. But in factories where labor-saving machinery has reached its most wonderful development, little children are at work; wherever the new

forces are anything like fully utilized, large classes are maintained by charity or live on the verge of recourse to it; amid
the greatest accumulations of wealth, men die of starvation,
and puny infants suckle dry breasts; while everywhere the
greed of gain, the worship of wealth, shows the force of
the fear of want. The promised land flies before us like the
mirage. The fruits of the tree of knowledge turn as we grasp
them to apples of Sodom that crumble at the touch.

It is true that wealth has been greatly increased, and that the
average of comfort, leisure, and refinement has been raised;
but these gains are not general. In them the lowest class do
not share. I do not mean that the condition of the lowest class
has nowhere nor in anything been improved; but that there
is nowhere any improvement which can be credited to
increased productive power. I mean that the tendency of
what we call material progress is in nowise to improve the
condition of the lowest class in the essentials of healthy,
happy human life. Nay, more, that it is still further to depress
the condition of the lowest class. The new forces, elevating
in their nature though they be, do not act upon the social
fabric from underneath, as was for a long time hoped and
believed, but strike it at a point intermediate between top
and bottom. It is as though an immense wedge were being
forced, not underneath society, but through society. Those
who are above the point of separation are elevated, but
those who are below are crushed down.

This depressing effect is not generally realized, for it is not
apparent where there has long existed a class just able to live.
Where the lowest class barely lives, as has been the case for a
long time in many parts of Europe, it is impossible for it to
get any lower, for the next lowest step is out of existence, and
no tendency to further depression can readily show itself. But
in the progress of new settlements to the conditions of older

communities it may clearly be seen that material progress does not merely fail to relieve poverty—it actually produces it.

This association of poverty with progress is the great enigma of our times. It is the central fact from which spring industrial, social, and political difficulties that perplex the world, and with which statesmanship and philanthropy and education grapple in vain. From it come the clouds that over-hang the future of the most progressive and self-reliant nations. It is the riddle which the Sphinx of Fate puts to our civilization, and which not to answer is to be destroyed. So long as all the increased wealth which modern progress brings goes but to build up great fortunes, to increase luxury and make sharper the contrast between the House of Have and the House of Want, progress is not real and cannot be permanent. The reaction must come. The tower leans from its foundations, and every new story but hastens the final catastrophe. To educate men who must be condemned to poverty, is but to make them restive; to base on a state of most glaring social inequality political institutions under which men are theoretically equal, is to stand a pyramid on its apex.

All-important as this question is, pressing itself from every quarter painfully upon attention, it has not yet received a solution which accounts for all the facts and points to any clear and simple remedy.

It must be within the province of political economy to solve it. For political economy is not a set of dogmas. It is the explanation of a certain set of facts. It is the science which, in the sequence of certain phenomena, seeks to trace mutual relations and to identify cause and effect, just as the physical sciences seek to do in other sets of phenomena. It lays its foundations upon firm ground. The premises from which it makes its deductions are truths which have the highest sanction; axioms which we all recognize; upon which we safely base the reasoning and actions of everyday life, and which may be reduced to the metaphysical expression of the physical law that motion seeks the line of least resistance—viz., that men seek to gratify their desires with the least exertion.

I propose in the following pages to attempt to solve by the methods of political economy the great problem I have outlined. I propose to seek the law which associates poverty with progress, and increases want with advancing wealth. Properly commenced and carefully pursued, such an investigation must yield a conclusion that will stand every test, and as truth, will correlate with all other truth. For in the sequence of phenomena there is no accident. Every effect has a cause, and every fact implies a preceding fact.

I propose in this inquiry to take nothing for granted, I propose to beg no question, to shrink from no conclusion, but to follow truth wherever it may lead.

2

POVERTY NOT DUE TO OVER-POPULATION

THAT VEGETABLE AND animal life tends to press against the limits of space does not prove the same tendency in human life. Granted that man is only a more highly developed animal; that the ring-tailed monkey is a distant relative who has gradually developed acrobatic tendencies, and the hump-backed whale a far-off connection who in early life took to the sea—granted that back of these he is kin to the vegetable, and is still subject to the same laws as plants, fishes, birds, and beasts. Yet there is still this difference between man and all other animals—he is the only animal whose desires increase as they are fed; the only animal that is never satisfied. The wants of every other living thing are uniform and fixed. The ox of to-day aspires to no more than did the ox when man first yoked him. The sea gull of the English Channel, who poises himself above the swift steamer, wants no better food or lodging than the gulls who circled round as the keels of Cæsar's galleys first grated on a British beach. Of all that nature offers them, be it ever so abundant, all living things save man can take, and care for, only enough to supply wants which are definite and fixed. The only use they can make of additional supplies or additional opportunities is to multiply.

But not so with man. No sooner are his animal wants satisfied than new wants arise. Food he wants first, as does the

9

beast; shelter next, as does the beast; and these given, his reproductive instincts assert their sway, as do those of the beast. But here man and beast part company. The beast never goes further; the man has but set his feet on the first step of an infinite progression—a progression upon which the beast never enters; a progression away from and above the beast.

The demand for quantity once satisfied, he seeks quality. The very desires that he has in common with the beast become extended, refined, exalted. It is not merely hunger, but taste, that seeks gratification in food; in clothes, he seeks not merely comfort, but adornment; the rude shelter becomes a house; the undiscriminating sexual attraction begins to transmute itself into subtle influences, and the hard and common stock of animal life to blossom and to bloom into shapes of delicate beauty. As power to gratify his wants increases, so does aspiration grow. Held down to lower levels of desire, Lucullus will sup with Lucullus; twelve boars turn on spits that Antony's mouthful of meat may be done to a turn; every kingdom of Nature be ransacked to add to Cleopatra's charms, and marble colonnades and hanging gardens and pyramids that rival the hills arise. Passing into higher forms of desire, that which slumbered in the plant and fitfully stirred in the beast, awakes in the man. The eyes of the mind are opened, and he longs to know. He braves the scorching heat of the desert and the icy blasts of the polar sea, but not for food; he watches all night, but it is to trace the circling of the eternal stars. He adds toil to toil, to gratify a hunger no animal has felt; to assuage a thirst no beast can know.

Out upon nature, in upon himself, back through the mists that shroud the past, forward into the darkness that overhangs the future, turns the restless desire that arises when the animal wants slumber in satisfaction. Beneath things, he seeks the law; he would know how the globe was forged and the stars were hung, and trace to their origins the springs of life. And, then, as the man develops his nobler nature, there arises the desire higher yet—the passion of passions, the hope of hopes—the desire that he, even he, may somehow aid in making life better and brighter, in destroying want and sin, sorrow and shame. He masters and curbs the animal; he turns his back upon the feast and renounces the place of power; he leaves it to others to accumulate wealth, to gratify pleasant tastes, to bask themselves in the warm sunshine of the brief day. He works for those he never saw and never can see; for a fame, or maybe but for a scant justice, that can only come long after the clods have rattled upon his coffin lid. He toils in the advance, where it is cold, and there is little cheer from men, and the stones are sharp and the brambles thick. Amid the scoffs of the present and the sneers that stab like knives, he builds for the future; he cuts the trail that progressive humanity may hereafter broaden into a highroad. Into higher, grander spheres desire mounts and beckons, and a star that rises in the east leads him on. Lo! the pulses of the man throb with the yearnings of the god—he would aid in the process of the suns!

Is not the gulf too wide for the analogy to span? Give more food, open fuller conditions of life, and the vegetable or animal can but multiply; the man will develop. In the one the expansive force can but extend existence in new numbers; in the other, it will inevitably tend to extend existence in higher forms and wider powers. Man is an animal; but he is an animal plus something else. He is the mythic earth-tree, whose roots are in the ground, but whose topmost branches may blossom in the heavens!

Look simply at the facts. Can anything be clearer than that the cause of the poverty which festers in the centers of civilization is not in the weakness of the productive forces? In countries where poverty is deepest, the forces of production are evidently strong enough, if fully employed, to provide for the lowest not merely comfort but luxury.

It is this very fact—that want appears where productive power is greatest and the production of wealth is largest—that constitutes the enigma which perplexes the civilized world, and which we are trying to unravel. Evidently the Malthusian theory, which attributes want to the decrease of productive power, will not explain it. That theory is utterly inconsistent with all the facts. It is really a gratuitous attribution to the laws of God of results which, even from this examination, we may infer really spring from the mal-adjustments of men.

3

LAND RENT GROWS AS
COMMUNITY DEVELOPS

LAND, LABOR, AND Capital are the factors of production. The term Land includes all natural opportunities or forces; the term Labor, all human exertion; and the term Capital, all wealth used to produce more wealth. In returns to these three factors is the whole produce distributed. That part which goes to land owners as payment for the use of natural opportunities is called Rent; that part which constitutes the reward of human exertion is called Wages; and that part which constitutes the return for the use of capital is called Interest. These terms mutually exclude each other. The income of any individual may be made up from any one, two, or all three of these sources; but in the effort to discover the laws of distribution we must keep them separate.

There must be land before labor can be exerted, and labor must be exerted before capital can be produced. Capital is a result of labor, and is used by labor to assist it in further production. Labor is the active and initial force, and labor is therefore the employer of capital. Labor can be exerted only upon land, and it is from land that the matter which it transmutes into wealth must be drawn. Land therefore is the condition precedent, the field and material of labor. The natural order is land, labor, capital.

Increasing population increases rent without reference to the natural qualities of land, for the increased powers of co-operation and exchange which come with increased population are equivalent to—nay, I think we can say without metaphor, that they give—an increased capacity to land.

I do not mean to say merely that, like an improvement in the methods or tools of production, the increased power which comes with increased population gives to the same labor an increased result, which is equivalent to an increase in the natural powers of land; but that it brings out a superior power in labor, which is localized on land—which attaches not to labor generally, but only to labor exerted on particular land; and which thus inheres in the land as much as any qualities of soil, climate, mineral deposit, or natural situation, and passes, as they do, with the possession of the land.

Here, let us imagine, is an unbounded savannah, stretching off in unbroken sameness of grass and flower, tree and rill, till the traveler tires of the monotony. Along comes the wagon of the first immigrant. Where to settle he cannot tell—every acre seems as good as every other acre. As to wood, as to water, as to fertility, as to situation, there is absolutely no choice, and he is perplexed by the embarrassment of richness. Tired out with the search for one place that is better than another, he stops—somewhere, anywhere—and starts to make himself a home. The soil is virgin and rich, game is abundant, the streams flash with the finest trout. Nature is at her very best. He has what, were he in a populous district, would make him rich; but he is very poor. To say nothing of the mental craving, which would lead him to welcome the sorriest stranger, he labors under all the material disadvantages of solitude. He can get no temporary assistance for any work that requires a greater union of strength than that afforded by his own family, or by such help as he can permanently keep.

Though he has cattle, he cannot often have fresh meat, for to get a beefsteak he must kill a bullock. He must be his own blacksmith, wagonmaker, carpenter, and cobbler—in short, a "jack of all trades and master of none." He cannot have his children schooled, for, to do so, he must himself pay and maintain a teacher. Such things as he cannot produce himself, he must buy in quantities and keep on hand, or else go without, for he cannot be constantly leaving his work and making a long journey to the verge of civilization; and when forced to do so, the getting of a vial of medicine or the replacement of a broken auger may cost him the labor of himself and horses for days. Under such circumstances, though nature is prolific, the man is poor. It is an easy matter for him to get enough to eat; but beyond this, his labor will suffice to satisfy only the simplest wants in the rudest way.

Soon there comes another immigrant. Although every quarter section of the boundless plain is as good as every other quarter section, he is not beset by any embarrassment as to where to settle. Though the land is the same, there is one place that is clearly better for him than any other place, and that is where there is already a settler and he may have a neighbor. He settles by the side of the first comer, whose condition is at once greatly improved, and to whom many things are now possible that were before impossible, for two men may help each other to do things that one man could never do.

Another immigrant comes, and, guided by the same attraction, settles where there are already two. Another, and another, until around our first comer there are a score of neighbors. Labor has now an effectiveness which, in the solitary state, it could not approach. If heavy work is to be done, the settlers have a log-rolling, and together accomplish in a day what singly would require years. When one kills a bullock, the others take part of it, returning when they kill, and thus they have fresh meat all the time. Together they hire a schoolmaster, and the children of each are taught for a fractional part of what similar teaching would have cost the first settler. It becomes a comparatively easy matter to send to the nearest town, for some one is always going. But there is less need for such journeys. A blacksmith and a wheelwright soon set up shops, and our settler can have his tools repaired for a small part of the labor it formerly cost him. A store is opened and he can get what he wants as he wants it; a post-office, soon added, gives him regular communication with the rest of the world. Then comes a cobbler, a carpenter, a harness-maker, a doctor; and a little church soon arises. Satisfactions become possible that in the solitary state were impossible. There are gratifications for the social and the intellectual nature—for that part of the man that rises above the animal. The power of sympathy, the sense of companionship, the emulation of comparison and contrast, open a wider, and fuller, and more varied life. In rejoicing, there are others to rejoice; in sorrow, the mourners do not mourn alone. There are husking bees, and apple parings, and quilting parties. Though the ballroom be unplastered and the orchestra but a fiddle, the notes of the magician are yet in the strain, and Cupid dances with the dancers. At the wedding, there are others to admire and enjoy; in the house of death, there are watchers; by the open grave, stands human sympathy to sustain the mourners. Occasionally, comes a straggling lecturer to open up glimpses of the world of science, of literature, or of art; in election times, come stump speakers, and the citizen rises to a sense of dignity and power, as the cause of empires is tried before him in the struggle of John Doe and Richard Roe for his support and vote. And, by and by, comes the circus, talked of months before, and opening to children whose horizon has been the prairie, all the realms of the imagination—princes and princesses of fairy tale, mail-clad crusaders and turbaned Moors, Cinderella's fairy coach, and the giants of nursery lore; lions such as crouched before Daniel, or in circling Roman amphitheater tore the saints of God; ostriches who recall the sandy deserts; camels such as stood around when the wicked brethren raised Joseph from the well and sold him into bondage; elephants such as crossed the Alps with Hannibal, or felt the sword of the Maccabees; and glorious music that thrills and builds in the chambers of the mind as rose the sunny dome of Kubla Khan.

Go to our settler now, and say to him: "You have so many fruit trees which you planted; so much fencing, such a well, a barn, a house—in short, you have by your labor added so much value to this farm. Your land itself is not quite so good. You have been cropping it, and by and by it will need manure. I will give you the full value of all your improvements if you will give it to me, and go again with your family beyond the verge of settlement." He would laugh at you. His land yields no more wheat or potatoes than before, but it does yield far more of all the necessaries and comforts of life. His labor upon it will bring no heavier crops, and, we will suppose, no more valuable crops, but it will bring far more of all the other things for which men work. The presence of other settlers—the increase of population—has added to the productiveness, in these things, of labor bestowed upon it, and this added productiveness gives it a superiority over land of equal natural quality where there are as yet no settlers. If no land remains to be taken up, except such as is as far removed from population as was our settler's land when he first went upon it, the value or rent of this land will be measured by the whole of this added capability. If, however, as we have supposed, there is a continuous stretch of equal land, over

which population is now spreading, it will not be necessary for
the new settler to go into the wilderness, as did the first. He
will settle just beyond the other settlers, and will get the
advantage of proximity to them. The value or rent of our
settler's land will thus depend on the advantage which it has,
from being at the center of population, over that on the verge.
In the one case, the margin of production will remain as
before; in the other, the margin of production will be raised.

Population still continues to increase, and as it increases so
do the economies which its increase permits, and which in
effect add to the productiveness of the land. Our first settler's
land, being the center of population, the store, the blacksmith's forge, the wheelwright's shop, are set up on it, or on
its margin, where soon arises a village, which rapidly grows
into a town, the center of exchanges for the people of the
whole district. With no greater agricultural productiveness
than it had at first, this land now begins to develop a productiveness of a higher kind. To labor expended in raising corn, or
wheat, or potatoes, it will yield no more of those things than
at first; but to labor expended in the subdivided branches of
production which require proximity to other producers, and,
especially, to labor expended in that final part of production,
which consists in distribution, it will yield much larger
returns. The wheat-grower may go further on, and find land
on which his labor will produce as much wheat, and nearly
as much wealth; but the artisan, the manufacturer, the storekeeper, the professional man, find that their labor expended
here, at the center of exchanges, will yield them much more
than if expended even at a little distance away from it; and
this excess of productiveness for such purposes the land owner
can claim just as he could an excess in its wheat-producing
power. And so our settler is able to sell in building lots a
few of his acres for prices which it would not bring for

wheat-growing if its fertility had been multiplied many times. With the proceeds, he builds himself a fine house, and furnishes it handsomely. That is to say, to reduce the transaction to its lowest terms, the people who wish to use the land build and furnish the house for him, on condition that he will let them avail themselves of the superior productiveness which the increase of population has given the land.

Population still keeps on increasing, giving greater and greater utility to the land, and more and more wealth to its owner. The town has grown into a city—a St. Louis, a Chicago, or a San Francisco—and still it grows. Production is here carried on upon a great scale, with the best machinery and the most favorable facilities; the division of labor becomes extremely minute, wonderfully multiplying efficiency; exchanges are of such volume and rapidity that they are made with the minimum of friction and loss. Here is the heart, the brain, of the vast social organism that has grown up from the germ of the first settlement; here has developed one of the great ganglions of the human world. Hither run all roads, hither set all currents, through all the vast regions round about. Here, if you have anything to sell, is the market; here, if you have anything to buy, is the largest and the choicest stock. Here intellectual activity is gathered into a focus, and here springs that stimulus which is born of the collision of mind with mind. Here are the great libraries, the storehouses and granaries of knowledge, the learned professors, the famous specialists. Here are museums and art galleries, collections of philosophical apparatus, and all things rare, and valuable, and best of their kind. Here come great actors, and orators, and singers, from all over the world. Here, in short, is a center of human life, in all its varied manifestations.

So enormous are the advantages which this land now offers for the application of labor that instead of one man with a span of horses scratching over acres, you may count in places thousands of workers to the acre, working tier on tier, on floors raised one above the other, five, six, seven, and eight stories from the ground, while underneath the surface of the earth engines are throbbing with pulsations that exert the force of thousands of horses.

All these advantages attach to the land; it is on this land and no other that they can be utilized, for here is the center of population—the focus of exchanges, the market place and workshop of the highest forms of industry. The productive powers which density of population has attached to this land are equivalent to the multiplication of its original fertility by the hundred fold and the thousand fold. And rent, which measures the difference between this added productiveness and that of the least productive land in use, has increased accordingly. Our settler, or whoever has succeeded to his right to the land, is now a millionaire. Like another Rip Van Winkle, he may have lain down and slept; still he is rich—not from anything he has done, but from the increase of population. There are lots from which for every foot of frontage the owner may draw more than an average mechanic can earn; there are lots that will sell for more than would suffice to pave them with gold coin. In the principal streets are towering buildings, of granite, marble, iron, and plate glass, finished in the most expensive style, replete with every convenience. Yet they are not worth as much as the land upon which they rest—the same land, in nothing changed, which when our first settler came upon it had no value at all.

That this is the way in which the increase of population powerfully acts in increasing rent, whoever, in a progressive country, will look around him, may see for himself. The process is going on under his eyes. The increasing difference in the productiveness of the land in use, which causes an increasing rise in rent, results not so much from the necessities of increased population compelling the resort to inferior land, as from the increased productiveness which increased population gives to the lands already in use. The most valuable lands on the globe, the lands which yield the highest rent, are not lands of surpassing natural fertility, but lands to which a surpassing utility has been given by the increase of population.

And where value seems to arise from superior natural qualities, such as deep water and good anchorage, rich deposits of coal and iron, or heavy timber, observation also shows that these superior qualities are brought out, rendered tangible, by population. The coal and iron fields of Pennsylvania, that to-day [1879] are worth enormous sums, were fifty years ago valueless. What is the efficient cause of the difference? Simply the difference in population. The coal and iron beds of Wyoming and Montana, which to-day are valueless, will, in fifty years from now, be worth millions on millions, simply because, in the meantime, population will have greatly increased.

It is a well-provisioned ship, this on which we sail through space. If the bread and beef above decks seem to grow scarce, we but open a hatch and there is a new supply, of which before we never dreamed. And very great command over the services of others comes to those who as the hatches are opened are permitted to say, "This is mine!"

4

LAND SPECULATION CAUSES
REDUCED WAGES

THERE IS A cause, not yet adverted to, which must be taken into consideration fully to explain the influence of material progress upon the distribution of wealth.

That cause is the confident expectation of the future enhancement of land values, which arises in all progressive countries from the steady increase of rent, and which leads to speculation, or the holding of land for a higher price than it would then otherwise bring.

We have hitherto assumed that the actual margin of cultivation always coincides with what may be termed the necessary margin of cultivation—that is to say, we have assumed that cultivation extends to less productive points only as it becomes necessary from the fact that natural opportunities are at the more productive points fully utilized.

This, probably, is the case in stationary or very slowly progressing communities, but in rapidly progressing communities, where the swift and steady increase of rent gives confidence to calculations of further increase, it is not the case. In such communities, the confident expectation of increased prices produces, to a greater or less extent, the effects of a combination among land holders, and tends to the withholding of land from use, in expectation of higher prices, thus forcing the margin of cultivation farther than required by the necessities of production.

In communities like the United States, where the user of land generally prefers, if he can, to own it, and where there is a great extent of land to overrun, this cause operates with enormous power.

The immense area over which the population of the United States is scattered shows this. The man who sets out from the Eastern seaboard in search of the margin of cultivation, where he may obtain land without paying rent, must pass for long distances through half-tilled farms, and traverse vast areas of virgin soil, before he reaches the point where land can be had free of rent—*i.e.,* by homestead entry or pre-emption. He (and, with him, the margin of cultivation) is forced so much farther than he otherwise need have gone, by the speculation which is holding these unused lands in expectation of increased value in the future. And when he settles, he will, in his turn, take up, if he can, more land than he can use, in the belief that it will soon become valuable; and so those who follow him are again forced farther on than the necessities of production require, carrying the margin of cultivation to still less productive, because still more remote points.

If the land of superior quality as to location were always fully used before land of inferior quality were resorted to, no vacant lots would be left as a city extended, nor would we find miserable shanties in the midst of costly buildings. These lots, some of them extremely valuable, are withheld from use, or from the full use to which they might be put, because their owners, not being able or not wishing to improve them, prefer, in expectation of the advance of land values, to hold them for a higher rate than could now be obtained from those willing to improve them. And, in consequence of this land being withheld from use, or from the full use of which it is capable, the margin of the city is pushed away so much farther from the center.

But when we reach the limits of the growing city—the actual margin of building, which corresponds to the margin of cultivation in agriculture—we shall not find the land purchasable at its value for agricultural purposes, as it would be were rent determined simply by present requirements; but we shall find that for a long distance beyond the city, land bears a speculative value, based upon the belief that it will be required in the future for urban purposes, and that to reach the point at which land can be purchased at a price not based upon urban rent, we must go very far beyond the actual margin of urban use.

That mineral land, when reduced to private ownership, is frequently withheld from use while poorer deposits are worked, is well known, and in new States it is common to find individuals who are called "land poor"—that is, who remain poor, sometimes almost to deprivation, because they insist on holding land, which they themselves cannot use, at prices at which no one else can profitably use it.

Whether we formulate it as an extension of the margin of production, or as a carrying of the rent line beyond the margin of production, the influence of speculation in land in increasing rent is a great fact which cannot be ignored in any complete theory of the distribution of wealth in progressive countries. It is the force, evolved by material progress, which tends constantly to increase rent in a greater ratio than progress increases production, and thus constantly tends, as material progress goes on and productive power increases, to reduce wages, not merely relatively, but absolutely.

The cause which limits speculation in commodities, the tendency of increasing price to draw forth additional supplies, cannot limit the speculative advance in land values, as land is a fixed quantity, which human agency can neither increase nor diminish; but there is nevertheless a limit to the price of land, in the minimum required by labor and capital as the condition of engaging in production. If it were possible continuously to reduce wages until zero were reached, it would be possible continuously to increase rent until it swallowed up the whole produce. But as wages cannot be permanently reduced below the point at which laborers will consent to work and reproduce, nor interest below the point at which capital will be devoted to production, there is a limit which restrains the speculative advance of rent. Hence speculation cannot have the same scope to advance rent in countries where wages and interest are already near the minimum, as in countries where they are considerably above it.

5

THE BASIC CAUSE OF POVERTY

THE GREAT PROBLEM, of which recurring seasons of industrial depression are but peculiar manifestations, is now, I think, fully solved, and the social phenomena which all over the civilized world appall the philanthropist and perplex the statesman, which hang with clouds the future of the most advanced races, and suggest doubts of the reality and ultimate goal of what we have fondly called progress, are now explained.

The reason why, in spite of the increase of productive power, wages constantly tend to a minimum which will give but a bare living, is that, with increase in productive power, rent tends to even greater increase, thus producing a constant tendency to the forcing down of wages.

Land being necessary to labor, and being reduced to private ownership, every increase in the productive power of labor but increases rent—the price that labor must pay for the opportunity to utilize its powers; and thus all the advantages gained by the march of progress go to the owners of land, and wages do not increase.

The simple theory which I have outlined (if indeed it can be called a theory which is but the recognition of the most obvious relations) explains this conjunction of poverty with wealth, of low wages with high productive power, of degradation amid enlightenment, of virtual slavery in political liberty.

It harmonizes, as results flowing from a general and inexorable law, facts otherwise most perplexing, and exhibits the sequence and relation between phenomena that without reference to it are diverse and contradictory.

It explains why improvements which increase the productive power of labor and capital increase the reward of neither.

It explains what is commonly called the conflict between labor and capital, while proving the real harmony of interest between them.

It cuts the last inch of ground from under the fallacies of protection, while showing why free trade fails to benefit permanently the working classes.

It explains why want increases with abundance, and wealth tends to greater and greater aggregations.

It explains the vice and misery which show themselves amid dense population, without attributing to the laws of the All-Wise and All-Beneficent defects which belong only to the short-sighted and selfish enactments of men.

The truth is self-evident. Put to any one capable of consecutive thought this question:

"Suppose there should arise from the English Channel or the German Ocean a No-man's land on which common labor to an unlimited amount should be able to make thirty shillings a day and which should remain unappropriated and of free access, like the commons which once comprised so large a part of English soil. What would be the effect upon wages in England?"

He would at once tell you that common wages throughout England must soon increase to thirty shillings a day.

And in response to another question, "What would be the effect on rents?" he would at a moment's reflection say that rents must necessarily fall; and if he thought out the next step he would tell you that all this would happen without any very large part of English labor being diverted to the new natural opportunities, or the forms and direction of industry being much changed; only that kind of production being abandoned which now yields to labor and to landlord together less than labor could secure on the new opportunities. The great rise in wages would be at the expense of rent.

Take now the same man or another—some hard-headed business man, who has no theories, but knows how to make money. Say to him: "Here is a little village; in ten years it will be a great city—in ten years the railroad will have taken the place of the stage coach, the electric light of the candle; it will abound with all the machinery and improvements that so enormously multiply the effective power of labor. Will, in ten years, interest be any higher?"

He will tell you, "No!"

"Will the wages of common labor be any higher; will it be easier for a man who has nothing but his labor to make an independent living?"

He will tell you, "No; the wages of common labor will not be any higher; on the contrary, all the chances are that they will be lower; it will not be easier for the mere laborer to make an independent living; the chances are that it will be harder."

"What, then, will be higher?"

"Rent; the value of land. Go, get yourself a piece of ground, and hold possession."

And if, under such circumstances, you take his advice, you need do nothing more. You may sit down and smoke your pipe; you may lie around like the lazzaroni of Naples or the leperos of Mexico; you may go up in a balloon, or down a hole in the ground; and without doing one stroke of work, without adding one iota to the wealth of the community, in ten years you will be rich! In the new city you may have a luxurious mansion; but among its public buildings will be an almshouse.

In all our investigation we have been advancing to this simple truth: That as land is necessary to the exertion of labor in the production of wealth, to command the land which is necessary to labor, is to command all the fruits of labor save enough to enable labor to exist. We have been advancing as through an enemy's country, in which every step must be secured, every position fortified, and every by-path explored; for this simple truth, in its application to social and political problems, is hid from the great masses of men partly by its very simplicity, and in greater part by widespread fallacies and erroneous habits of thought which lead them to look in every direction but the right one for an explanation of the evils which oppress and threaten the civilized world. And back of these elaborate fallacies and misleading theories is an active, energetic power, a power that in every country, be its political forms what they may, writes laws and molds thought— the power of a vast and dominant pecuniary interest.

But so simple and so clear is this truth, that to see it fully once is always to recognize it. There are pictures which, though looked at again and again, present only a confused labyrinth of lines or scroll work—a landscape, trees, or something of the kind—until once the attention is called to the fact that these things make up a face or a figure. This relation, once recognized, is always afterward clear.

It is so in this case. In the light of this truth all social facts group themselves in an orderly relation, and the most diverse phenomena are seen to spring from one great principle.

It is not in the relations of capital and labor; it is not in the pressure of population against subsistence, that an explanation of the unequal development of our civilization is to be found. The great cause of inequality in the distribution of wealth is inequality in the ownership of land. The ownership of land is the great fundamental fact which ultimately determines the social, the political, and consequently the intellectual and moral condition of a people. And it must be so. For land is the habitation of man, the storehouse upon which he must draw for all his needs, the material to which his labor must be applied for the supply of all his desires; for even the products of the sea cannot be taken, the light of the sun enjoyed, or any of the forces of nature utilized, without the use of land or its products. On the land we are born, from it we live, to it we return again—children of the soil as truly as is the blade of grass or the flower of the field. Take away from man all that belongs to land, and he is but a disembodied spirit. Material progress cannot rid us of our dependence upon land; it can but add to the power of producing wealth from land; and hence, when land is monopolized, it might go on to infinity without increasing wages or improving the condition of those who have but their labor. It can but add to the value of land and the power which its possession gives. Everywhere, in all times, among all peoples, the possession of land is the base of aristocracy, the foundation of great fortunes, the source of power. As said the Brahmins, ages ago—

"To whomsoever the soil at any time belongs, to him belong the fruits of it. White parasols and elephants mad with pride are the flowers of a grant of land."

6

THE REMEDY

POVERTY DEEPENS AS wealth increases, and wages are forced down while productive power grows, because land, which is the source of all wealth and the field of all labor, is monopolized. To extirpate poverty, to make wages what justice commands they should be, the full earnings of the laborer, we must therefore substitute for the individual ownership of land a common ownership.

The right of ownership that springs from labor excludes the possibility of any other right of ownership. If a man be rightfully entitled to the produce of his labor, then no one can be rightfully entitled to the ownership of anything which is not the produce of his labor, or the labor of some one else from whom the right has passed to him. For the right to the produce of labor cannot be enjoyed without the right to the free use of the opportunities offered by nature, and to admit the right of property in these is to deny the right of property in the produce of labor. When non-producers can claim as rent a portion of the wealth created by producers, the right of the producers to the fruits of their labor is to that extent denied.

A house and the lot on which it stands are alike property, as being the subject of ownership, and are alike classed by the law-yers as real estate. Yet in nature and relations they differ widely. The one is produced by human labor and belongs to the class in political economy styled wealth. The other is a part of nature, and belongs to the class in political economy styled land.

The essential character of the one class of things is that they embody labor, are brought into being by human exertion, their existence or non-existence, their increase or diminution, depending on man. The essential character of the other class of things is that they do not embody labor, and exist irrespective of human exertion and irrespective of man; they are the field or environment in which man finds himself; the storehouse from which his needs must be supplied, the raw material upon which, and the forces with which alone his labor can act.

The moment this distinction is realized, that moment is it seen that the sanction which natural justice gives to one species of property is denied to the other.

For as labor cannot produce without the use of land, the denial of the equal right to the use of land is necessarily the denial of the right of labor to its own produce. If one man can command the land upon which others must labor, he can appropriate the produce of their labor as the price of his permission to labor. The fundamental law of nature, that her enjoyment by man shall be consequent upon his exertion, is thus violated. The one receives without producing; the others produce without receiving. The one is unjustly enriched; the others are robbed.

Place one hundred men on an island from which there is no escape, and whether you make one of these men the absolute owner of the other ninety-nine, or the absolute owner of the soil of the island, will make no difference either to him or to them. In the one case, as the other, the one will be the absolute master of the ninety-nine—his power extending even to life and death, for simply to refuse them permission to live upon the island would be to force them into the sea.

Upon a larger scale, and through more complex relations, the same cause must operate in the same way and to the same end—the ultimate result, the enslavement of laborers, becoming apparent just as the pressure increases which compels them to live on and from land which is treated as the exclusive property of others.

Yet, it will be said: As every man has a right to the use and enjoyment of nature, the man who is using land must be permitted the exclusive right to its use in order that he may get the full benefit of his labor. But there is no difficulty in determining where the individual right ends and the common right begins. A delicate and exact test is supplied by *value*, and with its aid there is no difficulty, no matter how dense population may become, in determining and securing the exact rights of each, the equal rights of all.

The *value* of land, as we have seen, is the price of monopoly. It is not the absolute, but the relative, capability of land that determines its value. No matter what may be its intrinsic qualities, land that is no better than other land which may be had for the using can have no value. And the value of land always measures the difference between it and the best land that may be had for the using. Thus, the value of land expresses in exact and tangible form the right of the community in land held by an individual; and rent expresses the exact amount which the individual should pay to the community to satisfy the equal rights of all other members of the community.

Thus, if we concede to priority of possession the undisturbed use of land, taxing rent into the public treasury for the benefit of the community, we reconcile the fixity of tenure which is necessary for improvement with a full and complete recognition of the equal rights of all to the use of land.

Consider what rent is. It does not arise spontaneously from land; it is due to nothing that the land owners have done. It represents a *value created by the whole community*.

Let the land holders have, if you please, all that the possession of the land would give them in the absence of the rest of the community. But rent, the creation of the whole community, necessarily belongs to the whole community.

7

SIMPLICITY OF METHOD OF
INTRODUCING REMEDY

IT IS AN axiom of statesmanship, which the successful founders of tyranny have understood and acted upon—that great changes can best be brought about under old forms. We, who would free men, should heed the same truth. It is the natural method. When nature would make a higher type, she takes a lower one and develops it. This, also, is the law of social growth. Let us work by it. With the current we may glide fast and far. Against it, it is hard pulling and slow progress.

By making use of existing machinery, we may, without jar or shock, assert the common right to land *by appropriating rent by taxation*. We already take some rent in taxation. We have only to make some changes in our modes of taxation to take it all.

In form, the ownership of land would remain just as now. No owner of land need be dispossessed, and no restriction need be placed upon the amount of land any one could hold. For, rent being taken by the State in taxes, land, no matter in whose name it stood, or in what parcels it was held, would be really common property, and every member of the community would participate in the advantages of its ownership.

Now, insomuch as the taxation of rent, or land values, must necessarily be increased just as we abolish other taxes, we may put the proposition into practical form by proposing—

To Abolish All Taxation Save That Upon Land Values

As we have seen, the value of land is at the beginning of society nothing, but as society develops by the increase of population and the advance of the arts, it becomes greater and greater.

In every civilized country, even the newest, the value of the land taken as a whole is sufficient to bear the entire expenses of government. In the better developed countries it is much more than sufficient. Hence it will not be enough merely to place all taxes upon the value of land. It will be necessary, where rent exceeds the present governmental revenues, commensurately to increase the amount demanded in taxation, and to continue this increase as society progresses and rent advances. But this is so natural and easy a matter, that it may be considered as involved, or at least understood, in the proposition to put all taxes on the value of land. That is the first step, upon which the practical struggle must be made. When the common right to land is so far appreciated that all taxes are abolished save those which fall upon rent, there is no danger of much more than is necessary to induce them to collect the public revenues being left to individual land holders.

Wherever the idea of concentrating all taxation upon land values finds lodgment sufficient to induce consideration, it invariably makes way, but there are few of the classes most to be benefited by it, who at first, or even for a long time afterward, see its full significance and power. It is difficult for workingmen to get over the idea that there is a real antagonism between capital and labor. It is difficult for small farmers and homestead owners to get over the idea that to put all taxes on the value of land would be unduly to tax them. It is difficult for both classes to get over the idea that to exempt capital from taxation would be to make the rich richer, and the poor poorer. These ideas spring from confused thought. But behind ignorance and prejudice there is a powerful interest, which has dominated literature, education, and opinion. A great wrong always dies hard, and the great wrong which in every civilized country condemns the masses of men to poverty and want, will not die without a bitter struggle.

8

WHY A LAND-VALUE TAX IS BETTER THAN AN EQUAL TAX ON ALL PROPERTY

THE GROUND UPON which the equal taxation of all species of property is commonly insisted upon is that it is equally protected by the state. The basis of this idea is evidently that the enjoyment of property is made possible by the state—that there is a value created and maintained by the community, which is justly called upon to meet community expenses. Now, of what values is this true? Only of the value of land. This is a value that does not arise until a community is formed, and that, unlike other values, grows with the growth of the community. It exists only as the community exists. Scatter again the largest community, and land, now so valuable, would have no value at all. With every increase of population the value of land rises; with every decrease it falls. This is true of nothing else save of things which, like the ownership of land, are in their nature monopolies.

The tax upon land values is, therefore, the most just and equal of all taxes. It falls only upon those who receive from society a peculiar and valuable benefit, and upon them in proportion to the benefit they receive. It is the taking by the community, for the use of the community, of that value which is the creation of the community. It is the application of the common property to common uses. When all rent is taken by taxation for the needs of the community, then will the equality ordained by nature be attained. No citizen will have an advantage over any other citizen save as is given by his industry, skill, and intelligence; and each will obtain what he fairly earns. Then, but not till then, will labor get its full reward, and capital its natural return.

ALLEGED DIFFICULTY OF DISTINGUISHING LAND FROM IMPROVEMENTS

THE ONLY OBJECTION to the tax on rent or land values which is to be met with in standard politico-economic works is one which concedes its advantages—for it is, that from the difficulty of separation, we might, in taxing the rent of land, tax something else. McCulloch, for instance, declares taxes on the rent of land to be impolitic and unjust because the return received for the natural and inherent powers of the soil cannot be clearly distinguished from the return received from improvements and meliorations, which might thus be discouraged. Macaulay somewhere says that if the admission of the attraction of gravitation were inimical to any considerable pecuniary interest, there would not be wanting arguments against gravitation—a truth of which this objection is an illustration. For admitting that it is impossible invariably to separate the value of land from the value of improvements, is this necessity of continuing to tax *some* improvements any reason why we should continue to tax *all* improvements? If it discourage production to tax values which labor and capital have intimately combined with that of land, how much greater discouragement is involved in taxing not only these, but all the clearly distinguishable values which labor and capital create?

But, as a matter of fact, the value of land can always be readily distinguished from the value of improvements. In countries like the United States there is much valuable land that has never been improved; and in many of the States the value of the land and the value of improvements are habitually estimated separately by the assessors, though afterward reunited under the term real estate. Nor where ground has been occupied from immemorial times, is there any difficulty in getting at the value of the bare land, for frequently the land is owned by one person and the buildings by another, and when a fire occurs and improvements are destroyed, a clear and definite value remains in the land. In the oldest country in the world no difficulty whatever can attend the separation, if all that be attempted is to separate the value of the clearly distinguishable improvements, made within a moderate period, from the value of the land, should they be destroyed. This, manifestly, is all that justice or policy requires. Absolute accuracy is impossible in any system, and to attempt to separate all that the human race has done from what nature originally provided would be as absurd as impracticable. A swamp drained or a hill terraced by the Romans constitutes now as much a part of the natural advantages of the British Isles as though the work had been done by earthquake or glacier. The fact that after a certain lapse of time the value of such permanent improvements would be considered as having lapsed into that of the land, and would be taxed accordingly, could have no deterrent effect on such improvements, for such works are frequently undertaken upon leases for years. The fact is that each generation builds and improves for itself, and not for the remote future. And the further fact is that each generation is heir, not only to the natural powers of the earth, but to all that remains of the work of past generations.

10

EFFECT OF REMEDY UPON WEALTH PRODUCTION

THE ELDER MIRABEAU, we are told, ranked the proposition of Quesnay, to substitute one single tax on rent (the *impôt unique)* for all other taxes, as a discovery equal in utility to the invention of writing or the substitution of the use of money for barter.

To whosoever will think over the matter, this saying will appear an evidence of penetration rather than of extravagance. The advantages which would be gained by substituting for the numerous taxes by which the public revenues are now raised, a single tax levied upon the value of land, will appear more and more important the more they are considered. This is the secret which would transform the little village into the great city. With all the burdens removed which now oppress industry and hamper exchange, the production of wealth would go on with a rapidity now undreamed of. This, in its turn, would lead to an increase in the value of land—a new surplus which society might take for general purposes. And released from the difficulties which attend the collection of revenue in a way that begets corruption and renders legislation the tool of special interests, society could assume functions which the increasing complexity of life makes it desirable to assume, but which the prospect of political demoralization under the present system now leads thoughtful men to shrink from.

Consider the effect upon the production of wealth.

To abolish the taxation which, acting and reacting, now hampers every wheel of exchange and presses upon every form of industry, would be like removing an immense weight from a powerful spring. Imbued with fresh energy, production would start into new life, and trade would receive a stimulus which would be felt to the remotest arteries. The present method of taxation operates upon exchange like artificial deserts and mountains; it costs more to get goods through a custom house than it does to carry them around the world. It operates upon energy, and industry, and skill, and thrift, like a fine upon those qualities. If I have worked harder and built myself a good house while you have been contented to live in a hovel, the tax-gatherer now comes annually to make me pay a penalty for my energy and industry, by taxing me more than you. If I have saved while you wasted, I am mulct, while you are exempt. If a man build a ship we make him pay for his temerity, as though he had done an injury to the state; if a railroad be opened, down comes the tax-collector upon it, as though it were a public nuisance; if a manufactory be erected we levy upon it an annual sum which would go far toward making a handsome profit. We say we want capital, but if any one accumulate it, or bring it among us, we charge him for it as though we were giving him a privilege. We punish with a tax the man who covers barren fields with ripening grain; we fine him who puts up machinery, and him who drains a swamp. How heavily these taxes burden production only those realize who have attempted to follow our system of taxation through its ramifications, for, as I have before said, the heaviest part of taxation is that which falls in increased prices.

To abolish these taxes would be to lift the whole enormous weight of taxation from productive industry. All would be free to make or to save, to buy or to sell, unfined by taxes, unannoyed by the tax-gatherer. Instead of saying to the producer, as it does now, "The more you add to the general wealth the more shall you be taxed!" the state would say to the producer, "Be as industrious, as thrifty, as enterprising as you choose, you shall have your full reward! You shall not be fined for making two blades of grass grow where one grew before; you shall not be taxed for adding to the aggregate wealth."

And will not the community gain by thus refusing to kill the goose that lays the golden eggs; by thus refraining from muzzling the ox that treadeth out the corn; by thus leaving to industry, and thrift, and skill, their natural reward, full and unimpaired? For there is to the community also a natural reward. The law of society is, each for all, as well as all for each. No one can keep to himself the good he may do, any more than he can keep the bad. Every productive enterprise, besides its return to those who undertake it, yields collateral advantages to others. If a man plant a fruit-tree, his gain is that he gathers the fruit in its time and season. But in addition to his gain, there is a gain to the whole community. Others than the owner are benefited by the increased supply of fruit; the birds which it shelters fly far and wide; the rain which it helps to attract falls not alone on his field; and, even to the eye which rests upon it from a distance, it brings a sense of beauty. And so with everything else. The building of a house, a factory, a ship, or a railroad, benefits others besides those who get the direct profits.

Well may the community leave to the individual producer all that prompts him to exertion; well may it let the laborer have the full reward of his labor, and the capitalist the full return of his capital. For the more that labor and capital produce, the greater grows the common wealth in which all may share. And in the value or rent of land is this general gain expressed in a definite and concrete form. Here is a fund which the state may take while leaving to labor and capital their full reward. With increased activity of production this would commensurately increase.

And to shift the burden of taxation from production and exchange to the value or rent of land would not merely be to give new stimulus to the production of wealth; it would be to open new opportunities. For under this system no one would care to hold land unless to use it, and land now withheld from use would everywhere be thrown open to improvement.

The selling price of land would fall; land speculation would receive its death blow; land monopolization would no longer pay. Millions and millions of acres from which settlers are now shut out by high prices would be abandoned by their present owners or sold to settlers upon nominal terms. And this not merely on the frontiers, but within what are now considered well-settled districts.

And it must be remembered that this would apply, not merely to agricultural land, but to all land. Mineral land would be thrown open to use, just as agricultural land; and in the heart of a city no one could afford to keep land from its most profitable use, or on the outskirts to demand more for it than the use to which it could at the time be put would warrant. Everywhere that land had attained a value, taxation, instead of operating, as now, as a fine upon improvement, would operate to force improvement. Whoever planted an orchard, or sowed a field, or built a house, or erected a manufactory, no matter how costly, would have no more to pay in taxes than if he kept so much land idle. The monopolist of agricultural land would be taxed as much as though his land were covered with houses and barns, with crops and with stock. The owner of a vacant city lot would have to pay as much for the privilege of keeping other people off of it until he wanted to use it, as his neighbor who has a fine house upon his lot. It would cost as much to keep a row of tumble-down shanties upon valuable land as though it were covered with a grand hotel or a pile of great warehouses filled with costly goods.

Thus, the bonus that wherever labor is most productive must now be paid before labor can be exerted would disappear. The farmer would not have to pay out half his means, or mortgage his labor for years, in order to obtain land to cultivate; the builder of a city homestead would not have to lay out as much for a small lot as for the house he puts upon it; the company that proposed to erect a manufactory would not have to expend a great part of their capital for a site. And what would be paid from year to year to the state would be in lieu of all the taxes now levied upon improvements, machinery, and stock.

Consider the effect of such a change upon the labor market. Competition would no longer be one-sided, as now. Instead of laborers competing with each other for employment, and in their competition cutting down wages to the point of bare subsistence, employers would everywhere be competing for laborers, and wages would rise to the fair earnings of labor. For into the labor market would have entered the greatest of all competitors for the employment of labor, a competitor whose demand cannot be satisfied until want is satisfied—the demand of labor itself. The employers of labor would not have merely to bid against other employers, all feeling the stimulus of greater trade and increased profits, but against the ability of laborers to become their own employers upon the natural opportunities freely opened to them by the tax which prevented monopolization.

With natural opportunities thus free to labor; with capital and improvements exempt from tax, and exchange released from restrictions, the spectacle of willing men unable to turn their labor into the things they are suffering for would become impossible; the recurring paroxysms which paralyze industry would cease; every wheel of production would be set in motion; demand would keep pace with supply, and supply with demand; trade would increase in every direction, and wealth augment on every hand.

11

EFFECT OF REMEDY UPON THE SHARING OF WEALTH

BUT GREAT AS they thus appear, the advantages of a transference of all public burdens to a tax upon the value of land cannot be fully appreciated until we consider the effect upon the distribution of wealth.

Tracing out the cause of the unequal distribution of wealth which appears in all civilized countries, with a constant tendency to greater and greater inequality as material progress goes on, we have found it in the fact that, as civilization advances, the ownership of land, now in private hands, gives a greater and greater power of appropriating the wealth produced by labor and capital.

Thus, to relieve labor and capital from all taxation, direct and indirect, and to throw the burden upon rent, would be, as far as it went, to counteract this tendency to inequality, and, if it went so far as to take in taxation the whole of rent, the cause of inequality would be totally destroyed. Rent, instead of causing inequality, as now, would then promote equality. Labor and capital would then receive the whole produce, minus that portion taken by the state in the taxation of land values, which, being applied to public purposes, would be equally distributed in public benefits.

That is to say, the wealth produced in every community would be divided into two portions. One part would be distributed in wages and interest between individual producers, according to the part each had taken in the work of production; the other part would go to the community as a whole, to be distributed in public benefits to all its members. In this all would share equally—the weak with the strong, young children and decrepit old men, the maimed, the halt, and the blind, as well as the vigorous. And justly so—for while one part represents the result of individual effort in production, the other represents the increased power with which the community as a whole aids the individual.

Thus, as material progress tends to increase rent, were rent taken by the community for common purposes the very cause which now tends to produce inequality as material progress goes on would then tend to produce greater and greater equality.

Who can say to what infinite powers the wealth-producing capacity of labor may not be raised by social adjustments which will give to the producers of wealth their fair proportion of its advantages and enjoyments! With present processes the gain would be simply incalculable, but just as wages are high, so do the invention and utilization of improved processes and machinery go on with greater rapidity and ease.

But I shall not deny, and do not wish to lose sight of the fact, that while thus preventing waste and thus adding to the efficiency of labor, the equalization in the distribution of wealth that would result from the simple plan of taxation that I propose, must lessen the intensity with which wealth is pursued. It seems to me that in a condition of society in which no one need fear poverty, no one would desire great wealth—at least, no one would take the trouble to strive and to strain for it as men do now. For, certainly, the spectacle of men who have only a few years to live, slaving away their time for the sake of dying rich, is in itself so unnatural and absurd, that in a state of society where the abolition of the fear of want had dissipated the envious admiration with which the masses of men now regard the possession of great riches, whoever would toil to acquire more than he cared to use would be looked upon as we would now look on a man who would thatch his head with half a dozen hats.

And though this incentive to production be withdrawn, can we not spare it? Whatever may have been its office in an earlier stage of development, it is not needed now. The dangers that menace our civilization do not come from the weakness of the springs of production. What it suffers from, and what, if a remedy be not applied, it must die from, is unequal distribution!

Nor would the removal of this incentive, regarded only from the standpoint of production, be an unmixed loss. For, that the aggregate of production is greatly reduced by the greed with which riches are pursued, is one of the most obtrusive facts of modern society, while, were this insane desire to get rich at any cost lessened, mental activities now devoted to scraping together riches would be translated into far higher spheres of usefulness.

12

EFFECT OF REMEDY UPON
VARIOUS ECONOMIC CLASSES

When it is first proposed to put all taxes upon the value of land, all land holders are likely to take the alarm, and there will not be wanting appeals to the fears of small farm and homestead owners, who will be told that this is a proposition to rob them of their hard-earned property. But a moment's reflection will show that this proposition should commend itself to all whose interests as land holders do not largely exceed their interests as laborers or capitalists, or both. And further consideration will show that though the large land holders may lose relatively, yet even in their case there will be an absolute gain. For the increase in production will be so great that labor and capital will gain very much more than will be lost to private land ownership, while in these gains, and in the greater ones involved in a more healthy social condition, the whole community, including the land owners themselves, will share.

It is manifest, of course, that the change I propose will greatly benefit all those who live by wages, whether of hand or of head—laborers, operatives, mechanics, clerks, professional men of all sorts. It is manifest, also, that it will benefit all those who live partly by wages and partly by the earnings of their capital—storekeepers, merchants, manufacturers, employing or undertaking producers and exchangers of all sorts—from the peddler or drayman to the railroad or steamship owner—and it is likewise manifest that it will increase the incomes of those whose incomes are drawn from the earnings of capital.

Take, now, the case of the homestead owner—the mechanic, storekeeper, or professional man who has secured himself a house and lot, where he lives, and which he contemplates with satisfaction as a place from which his family cannot be ejected in case of his death. He will not be injured; on the contrary, he will be the gainer. The selling value of his lot will diminish—theoretically it will entirely disappear. But its usefulness to him will not disappear. It will serve his purpose as well as ever. While, as the value of all other lots will diminish or disappear in the same ratio, he retains the same security of always having a lot that he had before. That is to say, he is a loser only as the man who has bought himself a pair of boots may be said to be a loser by a subsequent fall in the price of boots. His boots will be just as useful to him, and the next pair of boots he can get cheaper.

So, to the homestead owner, his lot will be as useful, and should he look forward to getting a larger lot or having his children, as they grow up, get homesteads of their own, he will, even in the matter of lots, be the gainer. And in the present, other things considered, he will be much the gainer. For though he will have more taxes to pay upon his land, he will be released from taxes upon his house and improvements, upon his furniture and personal property, upon all that he and his family eat, drink, and wear, while his earnings will be largely increased by the rise of wages, the constant employment, and the increased briskness of trade. His only loss will be if he wants to sell his lot without getting another, and this will be a small loss compared with the great gain.

And so with the farmer. I speak not now of the farmers who never touch the handles of a plow, but of the working farmers who constitute such a large class in the United States—men who own small farms, which they cultivate with the aid of their boys, and perhaps some hired help, and who in Europe would be called peasant proprietors.

Paradoxical as it may appear to these men until they understand the full bearings of the proposition, of all classes above that of the mere laborer they have most to gain by placing all taxes upon the value of land. That they do not now get as good a living as their hard work ought to give them, they generally feel, though they may not be able to trace the cause. The fact is that taxation, as now levied, falls on them with peculiar severity. They are taxed on all their improvements—houses, barns, fences, crops, stock. The personal property which they have cannot be as readily concealed or undervalued as can the more valuable kinds which are concentrated in the cities. They are not only taxed on personal property and improvements, which the owners of unused land escape, but their land is generally taxed at a higher rate than land held on speculation, simply because it is improved. But further than this, all taxes imposed on commodities, fall on the farmer without mitigation.

The farmer would be a great gainer by the substitution of a single tax upon the value of land, because the taxation of land values would fall with greatest weight, not upon the agricultural districts, where land values are comparatively small, but upon the towns and cities where land values are high; whereas taxes upon personal property and improvements fall as heavily in the country as in the city. And in sparsely settled districts there would be hardly any taxes at all for the farmer to pay. For taxes, being levied upon the value of the bare land, would fall as heavily upon unimproved as

upon improved land. Acre for acre, the improved and cultivated farm, with its buildings, fences, orchard, crops, and
stock could be taxed no more than unused land of equal
quality. The result would be that speculative values would be
kept down, and that cultivated and improved farms would
have no taxes to pay until the country around them had
been well settled. In fact, paradoxical as it may at first seem
to them, the effect of putting all taxation upon the value
of land would be to relieve the harder working farmers of
all taxation.

But the great gain of the working farmer can be seen only
when the effect upon the distribution of population is considered. The destruction of speculative land values would tend
to diffuse population where it is too dense and to concentrate
it where it is too sparse; to substitute for the tenement house,
homes surrounded by gardens, and fully to settle agricultural
districts before people were driven far from neighbors to look
for land. The people of the cities would thus get more of
the pure air and sunshine of the country, the people of the
country more of the economies and social life of the city. If,
as is doubtless the case, the application of machinery tends to
large fields, agricultural population will assume the primitive
form and cluster in villages. The life of the average farmer is
now unnecessarily dreary. He is not only compelled to work
early and late, but he is cut off by the sparseness of population
from the conveniences, the amusements, the educational
facilities, and the social and intellectual opportunities that
come with the closer contact of man with man. He would be
far better off in all these respects, and his labor would be far
more productive, if he and those around him held no more
land than they wanted to use, while his children, as they grew
up, would neither be so impelled to seek the excitement of
a city nor would they be driven so far away to seek farms

of their own. Their means of living would be in their own hands, and at home.

In short, the working farmer is both a laborer and a capitalist, as well as a land owner, and it is by his labor and capital that his living is made. His loss would be nominal; his gain would be real and great.

In varying degrees is this true of all land holders. Many land holders are laborers of one sort or another. This measure would make no one poorer but such as could be made a great deal poorer without being really hurt. It would cut down great fortunes, but it would impoverish no one.

Wealth would not only be enormously increased; it would be equally distributed. I do not mean that each individual would get the same amount of wealth. That would not be equal distribution, so long as different individuals have different powers and different desires. But I mean that wealth would be distributed in accordance with the degree in which the industry, skill, knowledge, or prudence of each contributed to the common stock. The great cause which concentrates wealth in the hands of those who do not produce, and takes it from the hands of those who do, would be gone. The inequalities that continued to exist would be those of nature, not the artificial inequalities produced by the denial of natural law. The non-producer would no longer roll in luxury while the producer got but the barest necessities of animal existence.

13

EFFECT OF REMEDY UPON SOCIAL IDEALS

FROM WHENCE SPRINGS this lust for gain, to gratify which men tread everything pure and noble under their feet; to which they sacrifice all the higher possibilities of life; which converts civility into a hollow pretense, patriotism into a sham, and religion into hypocrisy; which makes so much of civilized existence an Ishmaelitish warfare, of which the weapons are cunning and fraud?

Does it not spring from the existence of want? Carlyle somewhere says that poverty is the hell of which the modern Englishman is most afraid. And he is right. Poverty is the open-mouthed, relentless hell which yawns beneath civilized society. And it is hell enough. The Vedas declare no truer thing than when the wise crow Bushanda tells the eagle-bearer of Vishnu that the keenest pain is in poverty. For poverty is not merely deprivation; it means shame, degradation; the searing of the most sensitive parts of our moral and mental nature as with hot irons; the denial of the strongest impulses and the sweetest affections; the wrenching of the most vital nerves. You love your wife, you love your children; but would it not be easier to see them die than to see them reduced to the pinch of want in which large classes in every highly civilized community live? The strongest of animal passions is that with which we cling to life, but it is an everyday occurrence in civilized societies for men to put poison to their mouths or pistols to their heads from fear of poverty, and for one who does this there are probably a hundred who have the desire, but are restrained by instinctive shrinking, by religious considerations, or by family ties.

From this hell of poverty, it is but natural that men should make every effort to escape. With the impulse to self-preservation and self-gratification combine nobler feelings, and love as well as fear urges in the struggle. Many a man does a mean thing, a dishonest thing, a greedy and grasping and unjust thing, in the effort to place above want, or the fear of want, mother or wife or children.

And out of this condition of things arises a public opinion which enlists, as an impelling power in the struggle to grasp and to keep, one of the strongest—perhaps with many men the very strongest—springs of human action. The desire for approbation, the feeling that urges us to win the respect, admiration, or sympathy of our fellows, is instinctive and universal. Distorted sometimes into the most abnormal manifestations, it may yet be everywhere perceived. It is potent with the veriest savage, as with the most highly cultivated member of the most polished society; it shows itself with the first gleam of intelligence, and persists to the last breath. It triumphs over the love of ease, over the sense of pain, over the dread of death. It dictates the most trivial and the most important actions.

Now, men admire what they desire. How sweet to the storm-stricken seems the safe harbor; food to the hungry, drink to the thirsty, warmth to the shivering, rest to the weary, power to the weak, knowledge to him in whom the intellectual yearnings of the soul have been aroused. And thus the sting of want and the fear of want make men admire above all things the possession of riches, and to become wealthy is to become respected, and admired, and influential. Get money—honestly, if you can, but at any rate get money! This is the lesson that society is daily and hourly dinning in the ears of its members. Men instinctively admire virtue and truth, but the sting of want and the fear of want make them even more strongly admire the rich and sympathize with the fortunate. It is well to be honest and just, and men will commend it; but he who by fraud and injustice gets him a million dollars will have more respect, and admiration, and influence, more eye service and lip service, if not heart service, than he who refuses it. The one may have his reward in the future; he may know that his name is writ in the Book of Life, and that for him is the white robe and the palm branch of the victor against temptation; but the other has his reward in the present. His name is writ in the list of "our substantial citizens"; he has the courtship of men and the flattery of women; the best pew in the church and the personal regard of the eloquent clergyman who in the name of Christ preaches the Gospel of Dives, and tones down into a meaningless flower of Eastern speech the stern metaphor of the camel and the needle's eye. He may be a patron of arts, a Mæcenas to men of letters; may profit by the converse of the intelligent, and be polished by the attrition of the refined. His alms may feed the poor, and help the struggling, and bring sunshine into desolate places; and noble public institutions commemorate, after he is gone, his name and his fame. It is not in the guise of a hideous monster, with horns and tail, that Satan tempts the children of men, but as an angel of light. His promises are not alone of the kingdoms of the world, but of mental and moral principalities and powers. He appeals not only to the animal appetites, but to the cravings that stir in man because he is more than an animal.

Give labor a free field and its full earnings; take for the benefit of the whole community that fund which the growth of the community creates, and want and the fear of want would be gone. The springs of production would be set free, and the enormous increase of wealth would give the poorest ample comfort. Men would no more worry about finding employment than they worry about finding air to breathe; they need have no more care about physical necessities than do the lilies of the field. The progress of science, the march of invention, the diffusion of knowledge, would bring their benefits to all.

With this abolition of want and the fear of want, the admiration of riches would decay, and men would seek the respect and approbation of their fellows in other modes than by the acquisition and display of wealth. In this way there would be brought to the management of public affairs, and the administration of common funds, the skill, the attention, the fidelity, and integrity that can now be secured only for private interests.

Shortsighted is the philosophy which counts on selfishness as the master motive of human action. It is blind to facts of which the world is full. It sees not the present, and reads not the past aright. If you would move men to action, to what shall you appeal? Not to their pockets, but to their patriotism; not to selfishness, but to sympathy. Self-interest is, as it were, a mechanical force—potent, it is true; capable of large and wide results. But there is in human nature what may be likened to a chemical force; which melts and fuses and overwhelms; to which nothing seems impossible. "All that a man hath will he give for his life"—that is self-interest. But in loyalty to higher impulses men will give even life.

It is not selfishness that enriches the annals of every people with heroes and saints. It is not selfishness that on every page of the world's history bursts out in sudden splendor of

noble deeds or sheds the soft radiance of benignant lives. It
was not selfishness that turned Gautama's back to his royal
home or bade the Maid of Orleans lift the sword from the
altar; that held the Three Hundred in the Pass of Thermopylæ,
or gathered into Winkelried's bosom the sheaf of spears; that
chained Vincent de Paul to the bench of the galley, or
brought little starving children, during the Indian famine,
tottering to the relief stations with yet weaker starvelings in
their arms. Call it religion, patriotism, sympathy, the enthu-
siasm for humanity, or the love of God—give it what name
you will; there is yet a force which overcomes and drives out
selfishness; a force which is the electricity of the moral universe; a force beside which all others are weak. Everywhere
that men have lived it has shown its power, and to-day, as
ever, the world is full of it. To be pitied is the man who has
never seen and never felt it. Look around! among common
men and women, amid the care and the struggle of daily
life, in the jar of the noisy street and amid the squalor where
want hides—every here and there is the darkness lighted
with the tremulous play of its lambent flames. He who has
not seen it has walked with shut eyes. He who looks may
see, as says Plutarch, that "the soul has a principle of
kindness in itself, and is born to love, as well as to perceive,
think, or remember."

The will within us is the ultimate fact of consciousness. Yet
how little have the best of us, in acquirements, in position,
even in character, that may be credited entirely to ourselves;
how much to the influences that have molded us. Who is
there, wise, learned, discreet, or strong, who might not, were
he to trace the inner history of his life, turn, like the Stoic
Emperor, to give thanks to the gods, that by this one and that
one, and here and there, good examples have been set him,

noble thoughts have reached him, and happy opportunities opened before him.

To remove want and the fear of want, to give to all classes leisure, and comfort, and independence, the decencies and refinements of life, the opportunities of mental and moral development, would be like turning water into a desert. The sterile waste would clothe itself with verdure, and the barren places where life seemed banned would ere long be dappled with the shade of trees and musical with the song of birds. Talents now hidden, virtues unsuspected, would come forth to make human life richer, fuller, happier, nobler. For in these round men who are stuck into three-cornered holes, and three-cornered men who are jammed into round holes; in these men who are wasting their energies in the scramble to be rich; in these who in factories are turned into machines, or are chained by necessity to bench or plow; in these children who are growing up in squalor, and vice, and ignorance, are powers of the highest order, talents the most splendid. They need but the opportunity to bring them forth.

Consider the possibilities of a state of society that gave that opportunity to all. Let imagination fill out the picture; its colors grow too bright for words to paint. Consider the moral elevation, the intellectual activity, the social life. Consider how by a thousand actions and interactions the members of every community are linked together, and how in the present condition of things even the fortunate few who stand upon the apex of the social pyramid must suffer, though they know it not, from the want, ignorance, and degradation that are underneath. Consider these things and then say whether the change I propose would not be for the benefit of every one— even the greatest land holder!

14

LIBERTY, AND EQUALITY OF OPPORTUNITY

THE TRUTH TO which we were led in the politico-economic branch of our inquiry is as clearly apparent in the rise and fall of nations and the growth and decay of civilizations, and it accords with those deep-seated recognitions of relation and sequence that we denominate moral perceptions. Thus are given to our conclusions the greatest certitude and highest sanction.

This truth involves both a menace and a promise. It shows that the evils arising from the unjust and unequal distribution of wealth, which are becoming more and more apparent as modern civilization goes on, are not incidents of progress, but tendencies which must bring progress to a halt; that they will not cure themselves, but, on the contrary, must, unless their cause is removed, grow greater and greater, until they sweep us back into barbarism by the road every previous civilization has trod. But it also shows that these evils are not imposed by natural laws; that they spring solely from social maladjustments which ignore natural laws, and that in removing their cause we shall be giving an enormous impetus to progress.

The poverty which in the midst of abundance pinches and imbrutes men, and all the manifold evils which flow from it, spring from a denial of justice. In permitting the monopolization of the opportunities which nature freely offers to all, we have ignored the fundamental law of justice—for, so far as we can see, when we view things upon a large scale, justice seems to be the supreme law of the universe. But by sweeping away this injustice and asserting the rights of all men to natural opportunities, we shall conform ourselves to the law—we shall remove the great cause of unnatural inequality in the distribution of wealth and power; we shall abolish poverty; tame the ruthless passions of greed; dry up the springs of vice and misery; light in dark places the lamp of knowledge; give new vigor to invention and a fresh impulse to discovery; substitute political strength for political weakness; and make tyranny and anarchy impossible.

The reform I have proposed accords with all that is politically, socially, or morally desirable. It has the qualities of a true reform, for it will make all other reforms easier. What is it but the carrying out in letter and spirit of the truth enunciated in the Declaration of Independence—the "self-evident" truth that is the heart and soul of the Declaration—*"That all men are created equal; that they are endowed by their Creator with certain inalienable rights; that among these are life, liberty, and the pursuit of happiness!"*

These rights are denied when the equal right to land—on which and by which men alone can live—is denied. Equality of political rights will not compensate for the denial of the equal right to the bounty of nature. Political liberty, when the equal right to land is denied, becomes, as population increases and invention goes on, merely the liberty to compete for employment at starvation wages. This is the truth that we have ignored. And so there come beggars in our streets and tramps on our roads; and poverty enslaves men who we boast are political sovereigns; and want breeds ignorance that our schools cannot enlighten; and citizens vote as their masters dictate; and the demagogue usurps the part of the statesman;

and gold weighs in the scales of justice; and in high places sit those who do not pay to civic virtue even the compliment of hypocrisy; and the pillars of the republic that we thought so strong already bend under an increasing strain.

We honor Liberty in name and in form. We set up her statues and sound her praises. But we have not fully trusted her. And with our growth so grow her demands. She will have no half service!

Liberty! it is a word to conjure with, not to vex the ear in empty boastings. For Liberty means Justice, and Justice is the natural law—the law of health and symmetry and strength, of fraternity and co-operation.

They who look upon Liberty as having accomplished her mission when she has abolished hereditary privileges and given men the ballot, who think of her as having no further relations to the everyday affairs of life, have not seen her real grandeur—to them the poets who have sung of her must seem rhapsodists, and her martyrs fools! As the sun is the lord of life, as well as of light; as his beams not merely pierce the clouds, but support all growth, supply all motion, and call forth from what would otherwise be a cold and inert mass all the infinite diversities of being and beauty, so is liberty to mankind. It is not for an abstraction that men have toiled and died; that in every age the witnesses of Liberty have stood forth, and the martyrs of Liberty have suffered.

We speak of Liberty as one thing, and of virtue, wealth, knowledge, invention, national strength, and national independence as other things. But, of all these, Liberty is the source, the mother, the necessary condition. She is to virtue what light is to color; to wealth what sunshine is to grain; to knowledge what eyes are to sight. She is the genius of invention, the brawn of national strength, the spirit of national independence. Where Liberty rises, there virtue grows,

wealth increases, knowledge expands, invention multiplies
human powers, and in strength and spirit the freer nation
rises among her neighbors as Saul amid his brethren—taller
and fairer. Where Liberty sinks, there virtue fades, wealth
diminishes, knowledge is forgotten, invention ceases, and
empires once mighty in arms and arts become a helpless prey
to freer barbarians!

Only in broken gleams and partial light has the sun of
Liberty yet beamed among men, but all progress hath she
called forth.

Liberty came to a race of slaves crouching under Egyptian
whips, and led them forth from the House of Bondage. She
hardened them in the desert and made of them a race of
conquerors. The free spirit of the Mosaic law took their
thinkers up to heights where they beheld the unity of God,
and inspired their poets with strains that yet phrase the highest
exaltations of thought. Liberty dawned on the Phœnician
coast, and ships passed the Pillars of Hercules to plow the
unknown sea. She shed a partial light on Greece, and marble
grew to shapes of ideal beauty, words became the instruments
of subtlest thought, and against the scanty militia of free cities
the countless hosts of the Great King broke like surges against
a rock. She cast her beams on the four-acre farms of Italian
husbandmen, and born of her strength a power came forth
that conquered the world. They glinted from shields of
German warriors, and Augustus wept his legions. Out of the
night that followed her eclipse, her slanting rays fell again on
free cities, and a lost learning revived, modern civilization
began, a new world was unveiled; and as Liberty grew, so
grew art, wealth, power, knowledge, and refinement. In the
history of every nation we may read the same truth. It was
the strength born of Magna Charta that won Crécy and
Agincourt. It was the revival of Liberty from the despotism of

the Tudors that glorified the Elizabethan age. It was the spirit that brought a crowned tyrant to the block that planted here the seed of a mighty tree. It was the energy of ancient freedom that, the moment it had gained unity, made Spain the mightiest power of the world, only to fall to the lowest depth of weakness when tyranny succeeded liberty. See, in France, all intellectual vigor dying under the tyranny of the Seventeenth Century to revive in splendor as Liberty awoke in the Eighteenth, and on the enfranchisement of French peasants in the Great Revolution, basing the wonderful strength that has in our time defied defeat.

Shall we not trust her?

In our time, as in times before, creep on the insidious forces that, producing inequality, destroy Liberty. On the horizon the clouds begin to lower. Liberty calls to us again. We must follow her further; we must trust her fully. Either we must wholly accept her or she will not stay. It is not enough that men should vote; it is not enough that they should be theoretically equal before the law. They must have liberty to avail themselves of the opportunities and means of life; they must stand on equal terms with reference to the bounty of nature. Either this, or Liberty withdraws her light! Either this, or darkness comes on, and the very forces that progress has evolved turn to powers that work destruction. This is the universal law. This is the lesson of the centuries. Unless its foundations be laid in justice the social structure cannot stand.

Our primary social adjustment is a denial of justice. In allowing one man to own the land on which and from which other men must live, we have made them his bondsmen in a degree which increases as material progress goes on. This is the subtle alchemy that in ways they do not realize is extracting from the masses in every civilized country the fruits of their weary toil; that is instituting a harder and more hopeless slavery in place of that which has been destroyed; that is bringing political despotism out of political freedom, and must soon transmute democratic institutions into anarchy.

It is this that turns the blessings of material progress into a curse. It is this that crowds human beings into noisome cellars and squalid tenement houses; that fills prisons and brothels; that goads men with want and consumes them with greed; that robs women of the grace and beauty of perfect womanhood; that takes from little children the joy and innocence of life's morning.

Civilization so based cannot continue. The eternal laws of the universe forbid it. Ruins of dead empires testify, and the witness that is in every soul answers, that it cannot be. It is something grander than Benevolence, something more august than Charity—it is Justice herself that demands of us to right this wrong. Justice that will not be denied; that cannot be put off—Justice that with the scales carries the sword. Shall we ward the stroke with liturgies and prayers? Shall we avert the decrees of immutable law by raising churches when hungry infants moan and weary mothers weep?

Though it may take the language of prayer, it is blasphemy that attributes to the inscrutable decrees of Providence the suffering and brutishness that come of poverty; that turns with folded hands to the All-Father and lays on Him the responsibility for the want and crime of our great cities. We degrade the Everlasting. We slander the Just One. A merciful man would have better ordered the world; a just man would crush with his foot such an ulcerous ant-hill! It is not the Almighty, but we who are responsible for the vice and misery that fester amid our civilization. The Creator showers upon us his gifts—more than enough for all. But like swine scrambling for food, we tread them in the mire—tread them in the mire, while we tear and rend each other!

In the very centers of our civilization to-day are want and suffering enough to make sick at heart whoever does not close his eyes and steel his nerves. Dare we turn to the Creator and ask Him to relieve it? Supposing the prayer were heard, and at the behest with which the universe sprang into being there should glow in the sun a greater power; new virtue fill the air; fresh vigor the soil; that for every blade of grass that now grows two should spring up, and the seed that now increases fifty-fold should increase a hundred-fold! Would poverty be abated or want relieved? Manifestly no! Whatever benefit would accrue would be but temporary. The new powers streaming through the material universe could be utilized only through land.

This is not merely a deduction of political economy; it is a fact of experience. We know it because we have seen it. Within our own times, under our very eyes, that Power which is above all, and in all, and through all; that Power of which the whole universe is but the manifestation; that Power which maketh all things, and without which is not anything made that is made, has increased the bounty which men may enjoy, as truly as though the fertility of nature had been increased. Into the mind of one came the thought that harnessed steam for the service of mankind. To the inner ear of another was whispered the secret that compels the lightning to bear a message round the globe. In every direction have the laws of matter been revealed; in every department of industry have arisen arms of iron and fingers of steel, whose effect upon the production of wealth has been precisely the same as an increase in the fertility of nature. What has been the result? Simply that land owners get all the gain.

Can it be that the gifts of the Creator may be thus misappropriated with impunity? Is it a light thing that labor should be robbed of its earnings while greed rolls in wealth—that the many should want while the few are surfeited? Turn to history, and on every page may be read the lesson that such wrong never goes unpunished; that the Nemesis that follows injustice never falters nor sleeps! Look around to-day. Can this state of things continue? May we even say, "After us the deluge!" Nay; the pillars of the state are trembling even now, and the very foundations of society begin to quiver with pent-up forces that glow underneath. The struggle that must either revivify, or convulse in ruin, is near at hand, if it be not already begun.

The fiat has gone forth! With steam and electricity, and the new powers born of progress, forces have entered the world that will either compel us to a higher plane or overwhelm us, as nation after nation, as civilization after civilization, have been overwhelmed before. It is the delusion which precedes destruction that sees in the popular unrest with which the civilized world is feverishly pulsing only the passing effect of ephemeral causes. Between democratic ideas and the aristocratic adjustments of society there is an irreconcilable conflict. Here in the United States, as there in Europe, it may be seen arising. We cannot go on permitting men to vote and forcing them to tramp. We cannot go on educating boys and girls in our public schools and then refusing them the right to earn an honest living. We cannot go on prating of the inalienable rights of man and then denying the inalienable right to the bounty of the Creator. Even now, in old bottles the new wine begins to ferment, and elemental forces gather for the strife!

But if, while there is yet time, we turn to Justice and obey her, if we trust Liberty and follow her, the dangers that now threaten must disappear, the forces that now menace will turn to agencies of elevation. Think of the powers now wasted; of the infinite fields of knowledge yet to be explored;

of the possibilities of which the wondrous inventions of this century give us but a hint. With want destroyed; with greed changed to noble passions; with the fraternity that is born of equality taking the place of the jealousy and fear that now array men against each other; with mental power loosed by conditions that give to the humblest comfort and leisure; and who shall measure the heights to which our civilization may soar? Words fail the thought! It is the Golden Age of which poets have sung and high-raised seers have told in metaphor! It is the glorious vision which has always haunted man with gleams of fitful splendor. It is what he saw whose eyes at Patmos were closed in a trance. It is the culmination of Christianity—the City of God on earth, with its walls of jasper and its gates of pearl! It is the reign of the Prince of Peace!

15

THE CROSS OF A NEW CRUSADE

MY TASK IS done.

Yet the thought still mounts. The problems we have been considering lead into a problem higher and deeper still. Behind the problems of social life lies the problem of individual life. I have found it impossible to think of the one without thinking of the other, and so, I imagine, will it be with those who, reading this book, go with me in thought; for, whatever be its fate, it will be read by some who in their heart of hearts have taken the cross of a new crusade. This thought will come to them without my suggestion; but we are surer that we see a star when we know that others also see it.

The truth that I have tried to make clear will not find easy acceptance. If that could be, it would have been accepted long ago. If that could be, it would never have been obscured. But it will find friends—those who will toil for it; suffer for it; if need be, die for it. This is the power of Truth.

Will it at length prevail? Ultimately, yes. But in our own times, or in times of which any memory of us remains, who shall say?

For the man who, seeing the want and misery, the ignorance and brutishness caused by unjust social institutions, sets himself, in so far as he has strength, to right them, there is disappointment and bitterness. So it has been of old time. So is it even now. But the bitterest thought—and it sometimes comes to the best and bravest—is that of the hopelessness of the effort, the futility of the sacrifice. To how few of those who sow the seed is it given to see it grow, or even with certainty to know that it will grow.

Let us not disguise it. Over and over again has the standard of Truth and Justice been raised in this world. Over and over again has it been trampled down—oftentimes in blood. If they are weak forces that are opposed to Truth, how should Error so long prevail? If Justice has but to raise her head to have Injustice flee before her, how should the wail of the oppressed so long go up?

But for those who see Truth and would follow her; for those who recognize Justice and would stand for her, success is not the only thing. Success! Why, Falsehood has often that to give; and Injustice often has that to give. Must not Truth and Justice have something to give that is their own by proper right—theirs in essence, and not by accident?

That they have, and that here and now, every one who has felt their exaltation knows. But sometimes the clouds sweep down. It is sad, sad reading, the lives of the men who would have done something for their fellows. To Socrates they gave the hemlock; Gracchus they killed with sticks and stones; and One, greatest and purest of all, they crucified. And in penury and want, in neglect and contempt, destitute even of the sympathy that would have been so sweet, how many in every country have closed their eyes? This we see.

But do we see it all?

I have in this inquiry followed the course of my own thought. When, in mind, I set out on it I had no theory to support, no conclusions to prove. Only, when I first realized the squalid misery of a great city, it appalled and tormented me, and would not let me rest, for thinking of what caused it and how it could be cured.

Political Economy has been called the dismal science, and as currently taught, *is* hopeless and despairing. But this, as we have seen, is solely because she has been degraded and shackled; her truths dislocated; her harmonies ignored; the word she would utter gagged in her mouth, and her protest against wrong turned into an indorsement of injustice. Freed, as I have tried to free her—in her own proper symmetry, Political Economy is radiant with hope.

For properly understood, the laws which govern the production and distribution of wealth show that the want and injustice of the present social state are not necessary; but that, on the contrary, a social state is possible in which poverty would be unknown, and all the better qualities and higher powers of human nature would have opportunity for full development.

And, further than this, when we see that social development is governed neither by a Special Providence nor by a merciless fate, but by law, at once unchangeable and beneficent; when we see that human will is the great factor, and that taking men in the aggregate, their condition is as they make it; when we see that economic law and moral law are essentially one, and that the truth which the intellect grasps after toilsome effort is but that which the moral sense reaches by a quick intuition, a flood of light breaks in upon the problem of individual life. These countless millions like ourselves, who on this earth of ours have passed and still are passing, with their joys and sorrows, their toil and their strivings, their aspirations and their fears, their strong perceptions of things deeper than sense, their common feelings which form the basis even of the most divergent creeds—their little lives do not seem so much like meaningless waste.

The scriptures of the men who have been and gone—the Bibles, the Zend Avestas, the Vedas, the Dhammapadas, and the Korans; the esoteric doctrines of old philosophies, the inner meaning of grotesque religions, the dogmatic constitutions of Ecumenical Councils, the preachings of Foxes, and Wesleys, and Savonarolas, the traditions of red Indians, and beliefs of black savages, have a heart and core in which they agree—a something which seems like the variously distorted apprehensions of a primary truth. And out of the chain of thought we have been following there seems vaguely to rise a glimpse of what they vaguely saw—a shadowy gleam of ultimate relations, the endeavor to express which inevitably falls into type and allegory. A garden in which are set the trees of good and evil. A vineyard in which there is the Master's work to do. A passage—from life behind to life beyond. A trial and a struggle, of which we cannot see the end.

Look around to-day.

Lo! here, now, in our civilized society, the old allegories yet have a meaning, the old myths are still true. Into the Valley of the Shadow of Death yet often leads the path of duty, through the streets of Vanity Fair walk Christian and Faithful, and on Greatheart's armor ring the clanging blows. Ormuzd still fights with Ahriman—the Prince of Light with the Powers of Darkness. He who will hear, to him the clarions of the battle call.

How they call, and call, and call, till the heart swells that hears them! Strong soul and high endeavor, the world needs them now. Beauty still lies imprisoned, and iron wheels go over the good and true and beautiful that might spring from human lives.